El Niño and La Niña

El Niño and La Niña

WEATHER IN THE HEADLINES

APRIL PULLEY SAYRE

Twenty-First Century Books
Brookfield, Connecticut

Our thanks to Mark Cane of Columbia University's Lamont-Doherty Earth Observatory for his scientific expertise.

Published by Twenty-First Century Books
A Division of The Millbrook Press, Inc.
2 Old New Milford Road
Brookfield, Connecticut 06804
www.millbrookpress.com   7/2002   18.68

Library of Congress Cataloging-in-Publication Data
Sayre, April Pulley.
El Niño and La Niña : weather in the headlines / April Pulley Sayre.
p. cm.
Includes bibliographical references and index.
Summary: Examines the El Niño and La Niña phenomena, why they occur, how meteorologists track them, how they affect global weather patterns, and their possible effect on global warming.
ISBN 0-7613-1405-9 (lib. bdg.)
1.   El Niño Current—Environmental aspects—Juvenile literature. 2. La Niña Current—Environmental aspects—Juvenile literature. 3. Global environmental change—Juvenile literature. [1. El Niño Current. 2. La Niña Current.] I. Title.
GC296.8.E4 S39 2000
551.6—dc21 00-025605

Cover photograph courtesy of AP/Wide World Photos

Photographs courtesy of Thomas Nebbia/NGS Image Collection: p. 10;
© Tom Nebbia/Corbis: p. 15; © National Geographic Society: pp. 17, 49, 52;
© Manfred Kage/Peter Arnold, Inc.: p. 20 (left); © Kjell B. Sandved/Visuals Unlimited: p. 20 (right); Liaison Agency: pp. 22 (© Paula Bronstein), 45 (© Gilles Mingasson); © Dr. Martin Wikelski: p. 24 (both); © Renzo Uccelli/Latin Focus.com: p. 27; AP/Wide World Photos: pp. 28, 33, 35, 38, 57; Science Source/Photo Researchers: pp. 37 (NASA/Goddard Space Flight Center/SPL), 47 (NOAA/SPL), 59 (NASA/SPL), 63 (© Hank Morgan); Reuters/Daniel Aguilar/Archive Photos: p. 41; NASA: p. 56; NOAA: p. 58; National Geophysical Data Center: pp. 66 (Edward Cook), 68 (Lonnie Thompson/Byrd Polar Research Center)

CONTENTS

1
WHEN THE WEATHER GOES WILD   **9**

2
PELICAN INVASIONS, DYING CORALS,
AND OTHER MARINE EVENTS   **19**

3
EL NIÑO IN SOUTH AMERICA   **26**

4
EL NIÑO IN NORTH AMERICA   **32**

5
EL NIÑO IN ASIA AND ELSEWHERE   **46**

6
LOOKOUT FOR LA NIÑA   **51**

7
THE SCIENCE OF TRACKING EL NIÑO   55

8
LOOKING BACK TO SEE THE FUTURE   65

~   ~

RESOURCES   73
GLOSSARY   75
INDEX   78

El Niño and La Niña

1
WHEN THE WEATHER GOES WILD

Floods. Droughts. Heavy snow storms. Dying coral reefs. Dry deserts that suddenly bloom. In 1997 and 1998, dramatic weather events and weather-related events were in the headlines almost every day. Weather in the Western Hemisphere seemed to have turned upside down. Dry places were suddenly rainy. Typically wet places were unusually dry. Cold places were warmer than usual. Peru received so much rain that a lake formed where none had been before!

Every year, some place has unusually heavy snow, or an unusually hot day, or an unexpectedly heavy rain. These variations in weather are natural. In 1997, however, the strange weather was linked to a change in climate—long-term weather. Climatologists, scientists who study climate, said these changes were caused by El Niño.

WHAT IS EL NIÑO?

El Niño is a natural shift in Pacific Ocean currents. It occurs irregularly, roughly every three to seven years. In an El Niño year, a large mass of warm seawater that is usually in the western Pacific Ocean shifts toward the central and eastern Pacific. This warm seawater spreads along the equator toward the region between Baja California and Peru. Water temperatures near Ecuador and Peru rise as much as 9°F (5°C) above normal.

Peruvian fishing boats were dry-docked in June 1983, when El Niño weather patterns kept warm currents close to shore. Fish were forced far out to sea, past the range of the fishing fleet.

What does warm water have to do with weather? Ocean temperatures and ocean currents affect the air above them. And air—or, more properly, the atmosphere—is where weather takes place. During an El Niño event, winds, ocean temperatures, and air pressure change in the Pacific region. El Niño and related shifts in environmental conditions change weather and climate in North America, Asia, Australia, and even Africa.

The term "El Niño" was first used by Peruvian fishermen who noticed that sometimes the cold current normally near Peru would disappear. Warm water would take its place, and fish would become scarce. At the same time, rains arrived in Peru and the plants grew quickly. Flowers bloomed profusely. These events were especially noticeable in December, near Christmas. For this reason, the fishermen called the sea and weather change El Niño, for the Christ Child. In certain years, the El Niño was particularly strong. Scientists now know that what the Peruvian fishermen observed is part of a widespread shift in the condition of the ocean and the atmosphere, the envelope of air surrounding Earth.

~ ~

SUN AND WIND AT WORK:
A NORMAL YEAR IN THE PACIFIC

Every day, the Sun warms water on the surface of the Pacific Ocean. In a normal year, strong winds called trade winds blow this warm surface water westward, where it puddles up near Asia. This piled up, warm ocean water actually makes the ocean 18 inches (45 centimeters) higher off the coast of Asia than it is off the coast of South America.

The warm water near Asia warms and moistens the air above it. This warm, moist air rises, creating monsoon rains that water southeast Asia and Australia. Meanwhile, on the other side of the Pacific, cold water from the deep ocean rushes upward to fill the space left by the heated water being pushed westward. This cold, nutrient-rich water makes for good fishing near Peru. But Peru receives very little rain, because the air, cooled by cold currents, does not rise and create storms.

~ ~

WHAT HAPPENS DURING AN EL NIÑO EVENT?

In an El Niño year, trade winds weaken or reverse direction. Warm seawater is no longer pushed westward. Instead, it sloshes back toward the Americas. The effect is similar to what happens when you slosh water one way, then back, in a bowl. The Pacific Ocean, however, is so huge that the surge of warm water takes ten weeks to reach South America. As it travels, the sun warms this surface water even more. The warm water pools in the central and eastern Pacific during El Niño.

The amount of warm water that pools in the central and eastern Pacific is tremendous. It covers an area one and a half times the size of the lower forty-eight United States and extends 109 yards (100 meters) below the surface. (Cold, deep ocean water lies below.) A million power plants could run for an entire year before they could heat up that much water.

Like a hot bath that steams up a bathroom, this pool of warm water evaporates easily, so it adds moisture to the air above it. In fact, it's constantly raining above this warm-water region. When blown inland, this moist air dumps rain onto the land. As a result, Peru experiences torrential rains, which fill its rivers and flood low-lying land. Meanwhile, southeast Asia and Australia, which usually experience monsoon rains, have dry weather instead.

~ ~

UNDER PRESSURE: THE SOUTHERN OSCILLATION

During an El Niño event, three major factors change in the Pacific region: wind direction, ocean temperature, and atmospheric (air) pressure. All three are connected in a cycle with no beginning and no end. They all influence one another, so it's impossible to say that any one begins a shift to El Niño conditions.

Atmospheric pressure is created by the weight of air above a given place pressing down on the air below. This pressure is measured using a barometer, and is often used in predicting approaching storms. All over Earth, air pressure is continually changing as the atmosphere is stirred by storms and winds, by hot air rising and cool air descending, and by weather systems jostling against one another. Changes in atmospheric pressure are part of the never-ending cycle of change in the atmosphere.

As an El Niño develops, atmospheric pressure increases to higher than normal over northern Australia and drops to abnormally low over Tahiti. Scientists call this atmospheric flip-flop that accompanies El Niño the Southern Oscillation. This change in the atmosphere, together with changes in ocean are called the El Niño Southern Oscillation (ENSO). But many journalists just call it El Niño, for short.

The shift in atmospheric pressure during El Niño is important because it affects weather and ocean currents. Wind is created when air rushes from a place of high pressure to a place of low pressure. A similar movement occurs when you let the air out of a balloon. The inside air, under great pressure, rushes out to where the air pressure is lower. Over the Pacific region, during El Niño, a shift in air pressure weakens or reverses trade winds. That change in wind direction lets warm water slosh back toward the Americas, creating the warm current noticed by Peruvians.

~ ~

WHAT IS LA NIÑA?

In 1998, as a very strong El Niño episode was ending, people began talking about a La Niña on the way. La Niña, which means "the girl," is the name given to conditions that are the opposite of those experienced in an El Niño. During a La Niña year, a pool of very *cold* water forms in the Pacific Ocean. Like El Niño, La Niña affects climate worldwide.

La Niña does not occur as often as El Niño, and does not always occur after an El Niño. Sometimes the ocean just switches from El Niño conditions to normal conditions. However, in 1998, a La Niña did follow an El Niño. In May 1998, water temperatures in the central and eastern Pacific cooled extremely quickly, dropping 15°F (8°C) in one month. Changes in climate were noticeable from California to Chile.

SHIFTING CLIMATE, SHIFTING SEAS

El Niño and La Niña are two extremes in naturally shifting oceanic and atmospheric conditions. This constant shifting has been described as "a seesaw," "a pendulum,"

June Anthony and Lloyd Wilmot help thirsty, drought-tamed elephants dig for water in Botswana during an El Niño-related drought.

OCEAN STRUCTURE IN DEPTH

Water deep in the ocean is very cold. Above it is warmer water. The division between the cold, deep ocean water and warmer surface water is called the thermocline.

In a normal year, the thermocline is closer to the surface in the eastern Pacific, along the South American coast, than in the western Pacific. In the western Pacific the thermocline may be 500 feet (152 meters) down, but only a third as deep in the eastern Pacific. Cold water wells up in the eastern ocean, creating cold currents, while warm surface water piles up in the western portion.

In a La Niña year, strong trade winds push even more warm water toward Asia. The thermocline tilts more steeply than in a normal year, deepening the western warm layer. To the east, more cold water comes even closer to the surface, and spreads westward, over the Central Pacific.

In an El Niño year, warm water sloshes eastward and the thermocline flattens out. Suddenly, the eastern Pacific has a thicker than usual layer of warm water, and cold water is farther from the surface than normal.

As you read about winds and currents, don't forget that the eastern Pacific lies against the west coast of the Americas—the western Pacific washes Asian shores.

The Pacific Ocean contains huge masses of warm and cool water. Movement of these masses has created El Niño conditions 31 percent of the time and La Niña conditions 23 percent of the time since 1950.

El Niño/Warming

As easterly trade winds decrease, warm water in the western Pacific flows eastward. The warm layer flows over cooler, nutrient-rich water, blocking the normal upwelling along the Americas. The thermocline is about 500 feet (152 meters) deep. Air along the coast of the Americas gains increased moisture from evaporation, so storms in the area increase.

Normal

Trade winds generally maintain a balance between warm western Pacific water and cool water in the eastern Pacific. The thermocline in the eastern Pacific is at 130 feet (40 meters), delivering cool, nutrient-rich water to the coast of the Americas.

La Niña/Cooling

Warm surface water is pushed westward by strong trade winds and flows toward Asia. Colder water upwells to the surface of the eastern Pacific. Evaporation is decreased in the eastern Pacific so there are fewer storms.

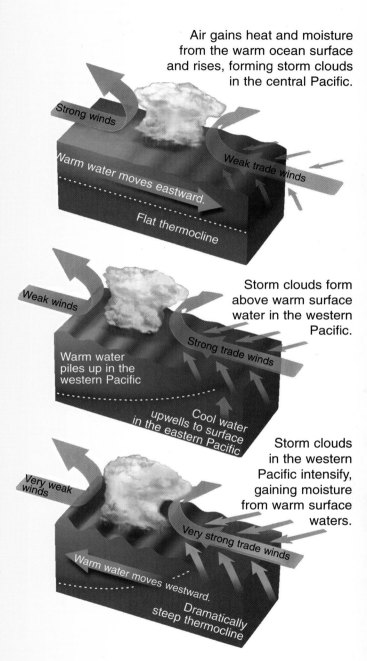

Air gains heat and moisture from the warm ocean surface and rises, forming storm clouds in the central Pacific.

Strong winds

Weak trade winds

Warm water moves eastward.

Flat thermocline

Storm clouds form above warm surface water in the western Pacific.

Weak winds

Strong trade winds

Warm water piles up in the western Pacific

Cool water upwells to surface in the eastern Pacific

Storm clouds in the western Pacific intensify, gaining moisture from warm surface waters.

Very weak winds

Very strong trade winds

Warm water moves westward.

Dramatically steep thermocline

or "a dance of two partners: ocean and atmosphere." In the past, people wondered if external factors, such as sunspots on the Sun, or earthquakes and volcanoes in the ocean, might cause El Niños and La Niñas. But now scientists understand that El Niños and La Niñas can occur just from the interaction of the ocean and the atmosphere.

El Niños and La Niñas vary in strength. At the time it occurred, the 1982–1983 El Niño was called the "Biggest El Niño of the Century," because it caused floods in California and Peru, wildlife die-offs on Pacific islands, and drought and famine in Africa and India. But then, along came an even stronger El Niño in 1997–1998. The El Niño of 1997–1998 was the strongest on record. In 1997 the mass of Pacific Ocean water warmed by El Niño was unusually warm and very large.

Worldwide, weather related to the 1997–1998 El Niño caused 2,100 deaths and $33 billion worth of property damage. But that was fewer deaths and less damage than might have occurred. Since 1982, scientists had been studying El Niño, and by 1997 they were able to predict it several months in advance. This gave individuals and governments some time to prepare for the El Niño weather and to avoid some of the potential damages.

2
PELICAN INVASIONS, DYING CORALS, AND OTHER MARINE EVENTS

In August 1997, thousands of pelicans invaded the town of Arica, Chile. They blocked traffic. They perched on buildings. They stole fish. Confused and starving, many of the birds died. In Arica and elsewhere along the coasts of Peru, Ecuador, and northern Chile, hundreds of thousands of seabirds died because they could not find food. Fish normally present off the coast of Peru and Ecuador had gone elsewhere. El Niño was to blame.

Normally, fish are abundant near Peru because of upwelling. An upwelling occurs when cold water from deep in the ocean rises to the surface. This nutrient-rich cold water fertilizes tiny floating ocean plants called phytoplankton. Those plants grow abundantly, the zooplankton (tiny animals) that eat them thrive, and the fish that eat zooplankton thrive, and the fish that eat other fish

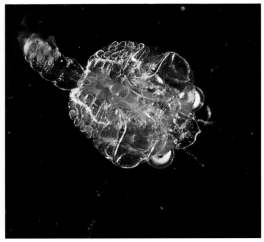

At left: An assortment of phytoplankton. At right: Zooplankton. This is a larval stage of a porcellanid crab.

do, too. The fish, in turn, are eaten by seabirds, sea lions, and people.

Because of this ocean food chain, Peru has one of the world's most productive fishing areas. Anchovies, which are small fish caught near Peru's shores, are ground up and used for fertilizer and as food for cows, pigs, and chickens. Much of this fish meal is shipped to the United States to be fed to livestock.

~ ~

BAD FISHING? BLAME IT ON EL NIÑO

When an El Niño occurs, cold, nutrient-rich water does not surface near Peru as usual. So, plankton and fish do not grow and reproduce abundantly offshore. Some fish die; others go elsewhere, following cold currents.

Peruvian fishing success plummets. During the El Niño of 1997–1998, Peruvian fishermen caught only about 20 percent of the amount of fish they normally do. Fishermen off southern Chile, however, had a good fishing year because fish swam to the cooler waters near their coast.

Swimming northward in warm water, tropical fish such as Mako sharks showed up in Monterey Bay, California, in 1997. Sport fishermen were thrilled to catch a marlin, a tropical fish, off the coast of Washington State that year. Bonito and albacore tuna, which are deep ocean fish, were found unusually near the California coast.

~ ~

STARVING WILDLIFE

During El Niño, fish-eating seabirds such as pelicans, cormorants, and albatrosses starve near Peru and Ecuador. Their chicks die because the parents cannot feed them. Eighty-five percent of the seabirds in Peru died during the El Niño of 1982–1983. In strong El Niño years, birds on the Galapagos Islands and other Pacific islands die by the millions.

Other fish eaters, such as fur seals, suffer, too. During the El Niño of 1997–1998, California sea lions, which are normally plump, were skinny. Squid and other fish they hunt swam deep into cooler waters, where they were difficult to reach. Undernourished female sea lions did not produce enough milk for their pups. An estimated 70 percent of California sea lion pups starved and died. Starving seabirds were found farther north, off the coasts of California and Oregon, as well.

**Sea lion pups are kept cool and wet by a volunteer of the
Friends of the Sea Lion in Laguna Beach, California. Many
sea lions died during the El Niño in 1997, but conservation
and rescue groups saved as many as possible.**

~ ~

TURNING UP THE HEAT ON CORAL REEFS

A coral is a tiny animal, smaller than your thumb. Yet
colonies of corals form tremendous reefs that stretch for
miles. The surface of the coral reef is a living skin of coral
animals that create the limestone reef below them, layer
by layer, year by year.

During El Niño years, the water temperature near Ecuador and South America rises and corals become ill. When the temperature rises, corals expel algae called zooxanthellae, that normally live inside them. The algae help the corals by photosynthesizing, producing food. Scientists call this damaged, empty coral "bleached" because it appears white. Bleached coral may recover if the temperature does not stay high for long. But in 1982, during a very strong El Niño, 97 percent of the reef corals near the Galapagos Islands died. The effects of the 1997–1998 El Niño on coral reefs have not yet been assessed. But the water surrounding the Galapagos, which normally is a maximum of 81°F (27°C) was 84°F (29°C) during that time. That's more than enough of a temperature increase to kill corals. Warm water near Australia killed many corals as well. Scientists are still waiting to see how much of the coral will recover.

~ ~

FAMINE AND FEAST IN THE GALAPAGOS

El Niño's effects are obvious in the Galapagos Archipelago, a group of nineteen islands and forty-two islets off the coast of Ecuador. Normally, the islands and nearby waters teem with wild animals: pelicans, blue-footed boobies, penguins, land iguanas, marine iguanas, sea lions, and even giant tortoises. Coral reefs offshore are frequented by brightly colored fish, octopuses, and sea stars.

But during an El Niño year, water temperatures near the Galapagos shift from cold to hot. Seaweed dies. Marine iguanas, which swim and dive to eat seaweed, go

El Niño in the Galápagos Islands spells disaster for life that depends on the sea, such as these marine iguanas (left), while increased rains mean land-based life flourishes, such as this Galapagos tortoise (right) wading through greenery.

hungry. Sea lions and seabirds starve because the fish are no longer available. Galapagos penguins, which can live near the equator only because of the cold currents, die in large numbers. In the 1982–1983 El Niño, a particularly strong one, 78 percent of Galapagos penguins died and 70 percent of the marine iguanas starved. Visitors to the Galapagos in 1997–1998 found a grim sight: beaches littered with carcasses of sea lions, birds, and marine iguanas.

Disaster for these animals, however, can be good for others. In 1997–1998, crabs, lava lizards, and hawks feasted on carcasses. Their populations thrived. El Niño brings rain that makes the naturally dry islands green with lush plant growth. Flowers bloomed, creating spectacular carpets of color on islands that are typically dry and desertlike. Plant eaters such as finches, giant tortoises, and land iguanas feasted on the lush growth. The finches reproduced quickly, nesting multiple times instead of just once in a season. So their populations increased drastically.

~ ~

It will take many years for the populations of sea lions and seabirds in hard-hit areas such as the Galapagos Islands to increase to their previous numbers. Yet as ocean conditions return to normal, these species can rebound, as long as another El Niño does not occur too soon, and as long as other dangers such as pollution, disease, habitat loss, or introduced species do not prevent their recovery. For thousands of years, animal populations have naturally fluctuated as El Niños have occurred.

3
EL NIÑO in SOUTH AMERICA

When it comes to El Niño, Peru is ground zero—not just for marine events, but also for changes in climate. El Niño's mass of warm seawater moves along the equator toward Peru, so the country strongly feels its effects. During an El Niño year, normally dry coastal Peru suddenly becomes rainy. From November 1997 to April 1998, Tumbes, Peru, received 74 inches (188 centimeters) of rainfall, twenty-six times more than normal! In some parts of the country rivers swelled and flooded, washing away roads, bridges, streets, and entire villages. Hillsides, soggy with rain, turned to liquid and mud slides covered homes, buried crops in the fields, and carried away cattle. Hundreds of people were killed and hundreds of thousands of people were left without homes. Northern Chile also received heavy rains. El Niño's effects, although strongest near Peru and Ecuador, were felt all the way to Brazil's Amazon rain forest.

In 1997, when Peru had more water than it could handle, Brazil and Guyana received less rain than normal. The dry weather was caused by El Niño's shift in weather patterns. Unfortunately, the drought created the perfect conditions for forest fires.

A LAKE IS BORN

So much rain fell in Peru that a temporary lake formed in what had been desert. The lake—which is 90 miles long, 20 miles wide, and 10 feet deep (145 kilometers long, 32 kilometers wide, and 3 meters deep)—will last for several years. The government has stocked the lake with fish, so people can use it for fishing—until it dries out.

NATURAL DISASTER—OR NOT?

The floods, fires, and mud slides of an El Niño year are usually considered natural disasters. But in some cases people's activities set the stage for fires, flood damage, and mud slides. By settling in valleys, close to rivers, people risk being in the path of floodwaters. A floodplain, the area where river water naturally spreads out during floods, is attractive for settlement because water is easily available and mud deposited by floods enriches the soil.

But living there is risky. Archaeologists have discovered that El Niño rains flooded a temple in about A.D. 1100. The Incas, who dominated Peru from the 1200s to the 1500s, built their cities atop hills and away from low-lying, flood-prone areas. Today, as human population

A fire in the Amazon rain forest near Apiau, Brazil. The drought associated with El Niño caused manmade fires to burn out of control.

increases, and land becomes scarce, more and more people are settling close to rivers.

Cutting down trees is another activity that can make El Niño damage worse. In Peru, hillsides that were deforested—stripped of trees—were noticeably more prone to mud slides in the El Niño of 1997–1998. Without trees to protect soil from pounding rains, and tree roots to hold soil in place, hillsides can quickly turn to mud.

Slash-and-burn farming is a problem, too. In order to clear forest in the Amazon, settlers normally cut down trees and burn the undergrowth. Then they plant crops. For a few years, the crops thrive, fertilized by the ash from burning, but soon the soil nutrients are used up, and farmers must move to another place to cut and burn again. Widespread slash-and-burn farming is a problem in any year. But El Niño–caused drought endangers the Amazon rain forest. Small fires, which would normally go out in the wet leaves of a rain forest can spread out of control. During the El Niño of 1997–1998, 19,000 square miles (49,210 square kilometers) of the Amazon rain forest burned—an area twice the size of Vermont!

Deforestation, slash-and-burn agriculture, and the placement of settlements in risky areas have had a hand in worsening the effects of so-called "natural disasters" not just in Peru, but worldwide.

≈ ≈

EL NIÑO CAN BE SICKENING

Weather related to El Niño brings an additional danger—disease. Areas that experience droughts often do not have enough water available for proper washing and hygiene.

Desperate for water, people end up using water from polluted lakes and rivers for drinking, cooking, and cleaning. Disease can spread quickly through these water sources.

Too much rain can also increase the spread of disease. Heavy rains overwhelm sewage systems, washing sewage into streets and into clean water sources. People left homeless by floods often must live crowded together in places where there is no clean water.

Rainy weather also creates conditions in which certain pests thrive. Warm standing water, left by heavy rains, is a breeding ground for mosquitoes. Mosquitoes can carry the diseases malaria and dengue fever. In 1997–1998, parts of Peru had three times the usual number of malaria cases, because standing water provided so much habitat for mosquitoes.

In the southwestern United States and southern Chile, rain causes lush grass growth. Mice and rats, which eat grass seeds, reproduce in large numbers. These animals can spread diseases such as the hantavirus. Such outbreaks occur months after the rains.

~ ~

BLOOMING AMAZING

El Niño is not all disaster. It brings unexpected blessings, too. In 1997 Chile's Atacama Desert bloomed. The Atacama Desert is a 600 mile- (968 kilometer-) ribbon of land that is usually barren sand dunes and pebbles, with very few plants. One of the driest places on earth, it receives less than an inch of rain in a normal year and parts of it may go without rain for twenty years. Yet in

1997 the Atacama received several inches of rain, thanks to El Niño. Plants quickly sprouted and grew. Soon, much of the desert was a field of flowers. Many of the flowers had not been seen for many decades! The seeds had been lying inactive in the soil but had sprouted when rain watered them. The great bloom of 1997 will undoubtedly be remembered for another hundred years or more. People may even wonder if it really happened, but photos will prove that it did.

4 EL NIÑO in NORTH AMERICA

In 1997–1998, American television news was filled with stories of disasters caused by El Niño. California was hit by heavy rains. Santa Monica, California, received so much rain that some bridges floated away. People in trucks and cars were washed into flooding rivers. Rescue workers in hovering helicopters plucked people from fast-flowing river water. A rain-soaked hillside turned into mud, flooding Rio Nido, California, and burying trees, houses, and cars. It seemed that every night more people devastated by El Niño were interviewed on TV.

El Niño changed weather over much of North America. But not all the changes were bad. While southern Californians suffered with wet weather, Chicagoans enjoyed an unusually warm winter. Midwestern flowers bloomed early. Minnesota residents played golf in February. Death Valley, California, had so much rain that the typically hot, dry desert bloomed with carpets of yellow and purple flowers.

RAIN, RAIN, RAIN

In late 1997, when word came that an El Niño was expected, Californians flocked to hardware stores. Tarps, sandbags, and roofing supplies sold out quickly. People cleaned their gutters to prepare for heavy rains. The city

Rescue workers dig out the bodies of two California Highway Patrol officers found inside their car, buried in mud in the Cuyama River near Santa Maria, California. The road collapsed into the river that had been swollen by an El Niño storm in February 1998.

of Los Angeles removed trees and debris from drainage channels built to carry excess water out of the city during storms.

It was a good thing that Californians prepared. In the winter of 1997–1998, southern California received more than twice its usual rainfall. It had its wettest February ever recorded. Storm after storm, heavy with warm, moist air, hit the California coast and Baja California. Streets in San Francisco flooded. In Laguna Beach heavy winter rains soaked hillsides, turning them to mud. On February 23, 1998, masses of flowing mud slammed into cliffside houses. Some people were in their living rooms one minute and in a river of mud the next. The mud pushed through the floors, walls, and windows of their collapsing houses, carrying buildings and people to the bottom of the hillside. People had to fight their way out of the deadly mud. Despite these disasters, many other people were spared the ravages of El Niño because they and local governments had prepared for the storms.

FOSSIL HUNTERS DIG EL NIÑO RAINS

Fossil hunters in southern California had their own reasons for welcoming the rains of El Niño. The heavy rain washed dirt off large areas. Fossils were exposed, and unusually easy to find. Near the Mojave Desert they found the bones of a 10-million-year-old whale, an ancient horse, and Gigantocamelus, a giraffelike camel.

~ ~

SURF'S UP, SNOW'S PLENTIFUL

Big storms bring big waves, whipped up by winds. In the 1997–1998 El Niño, storm waves as tall as three-story buildings hit the California coast. Stormy seas produced

Homes in Pacifica, California, were destroyed by an El Niño storm in May 1998.

unusually large waves that smashed the windows of sea-side restaurants in Cardiff, California. Waves carried away large chunks of the shoreline, causing some houses to fall into the sea.

What was disastrous weather for homeowners was a treat for surfers. Strong storms, fed by the moisture of El Niño, provided surfers with exciting waves in California and Mexico. Huntington Beach and Santa Cruz had waves twice the normal height. Someone even offered a $50,000 reward for the surfer who rode the tallest wave of the season! Surfers used their computers to access information from weather and marine reports in order to figure out which days would have the biggest waves, so they would know when to go to the beach.

Snow skiers had mixed reactions to El Niño. Ski resorts in the northern Rockies received less snow than normal, and had warmer, drier weather. But those in the southern Rockies had more snow. Some of the moisture that caused heavy rains in California also brought heavy snows to Lake Tahoe in California and Whistler ski resort in British Columbia. Of course, not everyone welcomed the snows, which can block roads and create avalanches.

~ ~

HURRICANE RISK, EAST AND WEST

Heavy rains and big waves weren't all the West Coast received. Hurricane Linda, the strongest storm ever recorded in the eastern North Pacific, hit Baja California with winds of 185 miles (298 kilometers) per hour. Hurricane Nora, 88 miles (142 kilometers) wide, threatened Los Angeles, although by the time it hit land its winds had diminished to below hurricane level. El Niño does not cause the Pacific hurricanes. But El Niño's moist, warm air can nourish hurricanes, allowing them to remain strong longer and travel farther north than they usually do. Another hurricane, Pauline, hit the west coast of Mexico in October 1997, damaging homes and businesses in Acapulco. But whether Hurricane Pauline was linked to El Niño is still uncertain.

Hurricane Linda approaches the mainland, September 12, 1997. Linda's northern tip is just passing over Cabo San Lucas, in Baja California Sur, Mexico. Winds toward the center reached 190 miles (306 kilometers) per hour, making Linda the strongest hurricane on record in the eastern Pacific. This image is a computer-generated reconstruction based on data from the American GOES-9 satellite.

In the Atlantic Ocean, El Niño decreases the number of hurricanes. During El Niño years, a high altitude river of wind called the jet stream shifts southward, over the southeastern United States. The jet stream's strong winds tend to break apart tropical storms and hurricanes in the Atlantic before they can move inland. As a result, Florida, the Gulf Coast, and the Caribbean Islands have less risk of hurricanes in El Niño years. During the 1997 hurricane season, there were only three Caribbean hurricanes, compared to the yearly average of six hurricanes.

Although Florida did not get hit by hurricanes in the winter of 1997–1998, it did get hit by tornadoes. At midnight on February 22, 1998, people in central Florida heard a terrible roaring noise. Seven tornadoes ripped

El Niño brought tornadoes to central Florida on February 23, 1998, killing at least thirty-three people and destroying hundreds of homes, including these in Kissimmee, Florida.

through, killing forty-two people, injuring several hundred others, and destroying eight hundred homes. The tornado winds ripped houses apart, wrapped mobile homes around pine trees, and sucked people out of houses onto their lawns. El Niño was partly to blame for these tornadoes because it strengthens the jet stream and shifts it southward, making strong storms more likely in the Southeast.

THE JET STREAM: GO WITH THE FLOW

Jet streams are currents of fast-moving air that circle Earth about 10 miles (16 kilometers) above the ground. They form where cold air from the poles meets warm air coming from near the equator. Jet streams push air masses around in the atmosphere, so they influence where storms occur.

Traveling from west to east, commercial pilots fly their planes up into the jet stream, which flows in that direction. Because the jet stream flows at speeds of 35 to 200 miles per hour (56 to 323 kilometers per hour) it can give a plane a push. This makes the trip faster and decreases fuel use. When flying east to west, pilots stay out of the jet stream because the strong headwind would slow them down.

During El Niño, a change in air pressure pulls the jet stream southward, across the southern United States. Strong storms form there, where cold and warm air clash. During a La Niña, the jet stream snakes widely. As a result, warm air can move farther north, and cold air can push south. This creates conditions which can spawn strong winter storms in the northern and western United States.

~ ~

WATER AND ICE

In 1997–1998, El Niño moisture was carried throughout the southern United States, from California to Florida. South Carolina, North Carolina, and Georgia were affected, too, receiving heavier than usual rains and strong storms. The unusually moist winter caused flooding, too. Sixteen inches (41 centimeters) of rain fell in two days in Jackson County, North Carolina. Rivers rose, flooding houses in North Carolina and Tennessee. Moist air pushed northward into New England and southeast Canada. Instead of receiving snow, these areas received freezing rain, which coated trees and power lines. Tree branches, heavy with ice, fell on houses and across power lines and roads. Many people lost electric power for days, some for weeks; the storm caused over $2 billion of damage in Canada alone.

~ ~

MEXICO ON FIRE

In June 1998, government officials told people in Texas to stay indoors as much as possible because heavy smoke from fires in Mexico was polluting the air outside. Mexican farmers were setting fires to clear weeds, old corn stalks, and undergrowth off the land before they planted crops. Marijuana growers and people illegally living in nature preserves were also setting fires to clear land. Like the fires in Brazil's Amazon rain forest, these fires spread out of control because of El Niño–caused drought.

During an El Niño, rains that move northward through Mexico from April to October may be delayed or not arrive at all. In 1998, during such a drought, 10,000 fires were set in Mexico, burning more than a half a million acres. Mostly, it was cropland. But ancient rain forests burned, too. One sixth of the Chimalapas rain forest, home to 1,500 rare species, was consumed by fire. Choking smoke from the fires drifted into the United States, creating a noticeable brown haze as far north as Chicago.

A Canadian helicopter pours water on a fire in the
Chimalapas forest, on the border of Oxaca and Chipas
in Mexico.

MARVELOUSLY MILD

In the United States, people have been keeping weather records for just over a century. By many measures, the winter of 1997–1998 was a record breaker. It was warmer and drier than usual in the midwestern United States and in much of Canada. Winnipeg, Canada, had temperatures 13°F (7°C) above normal for almost three months. Minnesota, Wisconsin, Illinois, Michigan, Ohio, Pennsylvania, and Connecticut had their warmest February ever. January and February 1998 were the warmest, wettest January and February ever recorded in the continental United States.

Because of the warm weather, cherry blossoms in Washington, D.C., bloomed early. In the mid-Atlantic states, heating bills were down by 25 percent or more in January. Meanwhile, in Minnesota, golfers were able to play on local courses in February, when normally the state would be covered by snow.

Winter sports enthusiasts weren't as thrilled by the warm weather. Snowmobilers and cross-country skiers were frustrated by the lack of snow. Some lakes did not freeze, so ice fishing was impossible. Warm winter weather really put a damper on the winter festival in Buffalo, New York. Snow, normally plentiful for the annual event, had to be trucked in!

A PHOTOGRAPHER'S DREAM AND BUGS, BUGS, BUGS

In most years, the Mojave and Sonora Deserts have colorful blooms in February and March, after seasonal rains. But the El Niño climate made the 1997–1998 bloom season more spectacular than usual. Mild temperatures and soaking rains caused the flowers to bloom earlier, and stay fresh for months instead of for just a few weeks. The searing heat that usually makes the flowers die back held off long enough for nature photographers to come from all over. Poppies, sand verbenas, desert primroses, and other flowers turned the deserts into colorful landscapes.

Even in the midwestern United States, spring wildflowers bloomed longer than usual. Flower lovers were able to see combinations of flowers that usually would not be seen together. Flowers that normally bloom at separate times bloomed so long that their seasons overlapped. Meanwhile, gardeners were glad to have the mild weather to get out and work in their gardens. Peas, spinach, and other plants grew earlier and better than usual.

El Niño brought rains, a mild winter, and a warm spring to the southwestern United States. But it also brought something else: insects. Rain conditions made grasses grow, producing plenty of food. Many insects began reproducing early because of the warmth, and were not killed off by cold temperatures. As a result, some towns in Colorado, Nevada, Arizona, and California were invaded by incredible numbers of grasshoppers, flies, silverfish, termites, and other insects.

~ ~

COPING WITH EL NIÑO DISASTERS
The El Niño of 1997–1998 may have had some pleasant effects, such as wildflower blooms and mild winter weather, but many people were left homeless, or with heavily damaged homes. They faced the process of recovering and rebuilding after disaster.

When disaster strikes, the United States government usually declares a county a disaster area and flies in equipment and supplies to help people cope with food shortages and loss of homes and businesses. Later, the Federal Emergency Management Administration may offer low-interest loans to help people recover and rebuild after disasters. This kind of aid helps, but recovery can be a very slow and difficult process.

SHOULD WE REBUILD?

After a disaster, many people's first instinct is to rebuild what they lost. But does it make sense to rebuild where mud slides are possible, on cliffs that can collapse, or in low-lying areas where floods can occur? Living in such places is risky. Yet people often rebuild there even after disasters, because it's the only land they own, or they love the location. Their family may have lived there for years. They may enjoy the view of a creek, a mountain gorge, or the sea.

In a way, that's the homeowner's business and his or her risk. But in another way, it may be yours, too. Most people in risky areas purchase Federal Flood Insurance, which is relatively low-cost insurance offered by the U.S. government. The government subsidizes this program, paying for some of the cost of houses damaged by ocean waves, lakeshore erosion, and flooding rivers.

Lately, many citizens are questioning whether the government should subsidize this program. It encourages people to crowd close to rivers, seashores, and lakeshores, destroying environmentally sensitive areas. It's a costly program. It also gives people an incentive to build and rebuild in places where perhaps houses should not have been built in the first place.

Consider, for instance, some of the luxury homes along the California coast. The homeowners know that someday the seashore will likely erode, and their houses will fall into the ocean.

Crews try to protect beachfront homes in Southern California with rock barriers.

But it's hard to think decades ahead, and the view is so beautiful, so they buy the house anyway. What does it matter if it falls into the sea? It may be heart-breaking, but the damages will be covered by federal insurance, and the house can be rebuilt there or somewhere else. Meanwhile, citizens all over the United States help pay for that new house, through the taxes they pay. When El Niño recurs, as it surely will, people in flood-prone, erosion-prone areas are likely to face trouble once again.

5
EL NIÑO in ASIA and ELSEWHERE

In 1997, so many fires were burning in parts of Indonesia that smoke filled the sky. Cars turned on their headlights because it was hard to see, even at noon. Cars and ships crashed. Children in schools couldn't see blackboards through the smoke. Millions of people developed lung problems, wheezing in the polluted air. The smoky haze spread to Malaysia, Singapore, Thailand, and the Philippines and lasted for four months. This air pollution wasn't directly caused by El Niño, but El Niño was partly to blame. El Niño's impacts were felt not only in Asia, but also in Australia and Africa.

~ ~

CHOKING ON SMOKE IN INDONESIA
Slash-and-burn agriculture, which is such a problem in the Amazon, causes trouble in Southeast Asia, too. Each year, people in Southeast Asia set fires to clear under-

This September 22, 1997, satellite image shows clouds of smoke from forest fires in Indonesian Borneo, at center. The Philippines is at upper right.

brush off land before they plant crops. The individual fires usually do not burn very large areas because the fires go out quickly in the moist leaves. Yearly rains also help put out the fires. But in August through November of 1997, the fires did not diminish in Indonesia; they burned out of control. Trees, vines, shrubs, and soil were dry because of an El Niño–caused drought. The rains that normally arrive in these months came late.

Small farmers and large companies made the problem worse. They took advantage of the dry conditions to clear and burn large areas of land in order to expand the planting of rice, oil palms, and pulpwood. Fires raged for months and could not be put out. Hundreds of thousands of acres of tropical rain forest were destroyed, including habitat for orangutans and Sumatran tigers. Japan, Britain, Australia, the United States, and other countries sent money, equipment, and firefighters to help put out the fires. But at the same time, even more fires were being set. It was mostly the rains, in November 1997, that helped douse the flames. Some people declared the four months of fires and choking smoke "Asia's largest man-made environmental disaster ever."

Even after the rains, the drought lingered. People in Java and Irian Jaya, which are part of Indonesia, suffered from lack of food and drinking water. So did people in Papua New Guinea. Crops dried out and died. Ponds and streams where people fished dried up and people went hungry.

~ ~

BEYOND THE PACIFIC: TELECONNECTIONS
It's easy to understand why El Niño affects Indonesia and Japan; those countries border the Pacific Ocean, where El Niño's pool of warm water forms. But scientists are still

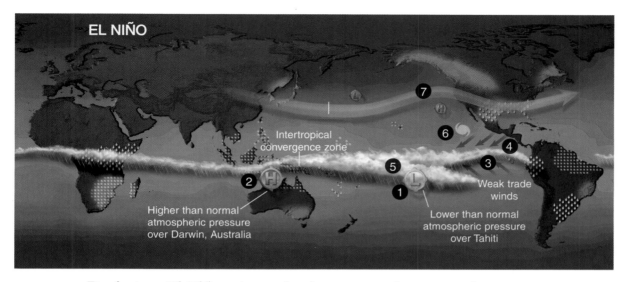

EL NIÑO

Intertropical convergence zone

Higher than normal atmospheric pressure over Darwin, Australia

Lower than normal atmospheric pressure over Tahiti

Weak trade winds

During an El Niño, atmospheric pressure becomes abnormally low near Tahiti (1) and unusually high over northern Australia (2). With the presence of the high-pressure system, Pacific trade winds that usually blow west weaken (3), allowing sun-warmed surface water to move eastward. This creates a warm band of water across the equatorial Pacific (4). Converging winds and warm water make more clouds than normal (5) and the subtropical jet stream, pulled south by the low over Tahiti, carries Pacific clouds eastward, producing more storms (6). As the jet stream continues east (7), it disrupts westbound Atlantic storms, reducing the number of hurricanes.

puzzling over some of the changes in climate that occur elsewhere during El Niño years. These long distance effects, linked to El Niño, are called teleconnections.

During El Niño years, the Indian Ocean heats up and the winds over it shift. Moist, warm water that is usually near India and southern Africa moves toward western

Australia. Areas of high and low atmospheric pressure shift, as they do in the Pacific Ocean. Scientists aren't sure why these changes occur or how they are connected to the warming in the Pacific Ocean. But as a result, India and southern Africa generally experience droughts in El Niño years. In 1982–1983 crops failed, grasses died, livestock starved, and people went hungry in southern Africa and India.

During the El Niño of 1997–1998, however, India, which was expected to experience a severe drought, had a better season than expected. The monsoons, the heavy seasonal rains that water India, came a few weeks later than normal, but dropped enough rain to water crops and keep fire damage minimal.

Eastern Australia was affected by drought as scientists expected. However, this drought did not bring the disastrous crop losses and cattle deaths that were predicted. Just enough rain fell when it was badly needed. As a result, the wheat crop and the cattle survived.

Meanwhile, farmers in southern Africa were expecting a drought, so many did not plant crops. Yet the rain came anyway, and the farmers wished they had planted. Because not enough food was planted, some people went hungry. East Africa even had unusually heavy rains and flooding, not drought!

Obviously, scientists still have much to learn about how El Niño impacts distant regions of Earth. It's much easier to predict how El Niño will affect areas bordering the Pacific Ocean, where the pool of warm water lies. Farther from that current, El Niño's impacts may be tempered by other powerful climatic systems. Each El Niño and La Niña event is different, and their effects play out in different ways.

6 LOOKOUT FOR LA NIÑA

In 1998, just when El Niño had ended, people braced for more odd weather. La Niña was on the way. A La Niña, which means "the girl," occurs when water in the eastern Pacific is cooler than normal and extends farther west than normal. These conditions can last for nine months to as much as two years. La Niña sea conditions are very nearly the mirror image of those in an El Niño year. Like an El Niño, a La Niña is an extreme—part of the central Pacific Ocean's natural fluctuation from very warm to normal to very cold.

~ ~

MYSTERIOUS LA NIÑA TURNABOUTS
La Niña—also called El Viejo ("the old man"), anti-El Niño, or a cold event—is not as well studied as El Niño. In general, during a La Niña, atmospheric pressure is

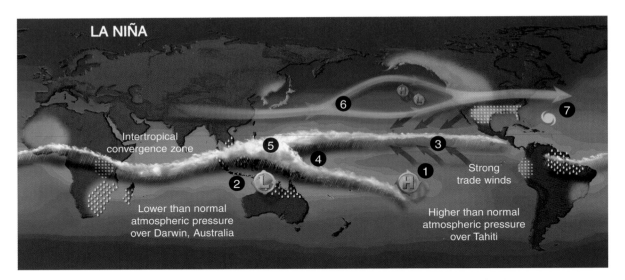

LA NIÑA

Intertropical
convergence zone

Lower than normal
atmospheric pressure
over Darwin, Australia

Strong
trade winds

Higher than normal
atmospheric pressure
over Tahiti

In the reverse of conditions of an El Niño year, La Niña is indicated by abnormally high pressure over Tahiti (1) and a low over northern Australia (2). Westbound trade winds become quite strong (3), moving sun-warmed surface water far west (4). Equatorial clouds split around the Tahiti high (5) and the subtropical jet stream is also weakened (6), allowing Atlantic hurricanes to move west and gather strength (7).

unusually high over Tahiti and unusually low over Australia, the reverse of conditions during an El Niño. Because of this change in atmospheric pressure, trade winds blowing westward strengthen and push cold surface waters near Peru farther than normal into the central Pacific. More cold water, from deep in the ocean, rushes upward to fill in the eastern Pacific, creating a very strong cold upwelling. During La Niña, the upwelling is so intense that cold water spreading into the central Pacific drops water temperatures near the equator.

La Niña's effects are generally the opposite of those during an El Niño year. Peru and Chile, which are very wet during an El Niño year, receive very little rain. Atlantic hurricanes, which are less common and weaker during an El Niño year, instead hit full force.

Like El Niño, La Niña shifts the jet stream. La Niña causes the jet stream to curve and snake dramatically, allowing cold air far to the south and warm air far to the north. This leads to stormy winters and can cause tornado formation. Dry conditions hit southern California and the southeastern United States. The northern United States and western Canada generally experience a colder, wetter winter than normal, while the South experiences a warm winter.

Australia and Indonesia, which have droughts during El Niño years, have wetter than normal years during La Niña. Although this moisture may help crops grow, it can also cause disaster. During the El Niño of 1997–1998, droughts and drought-related fires left much of the land bare of trees and plants. When La Niña arrived in 1998–1999, heavy rains caused mud slides in Indonesia because there were so few plants left to hold soil in place. So the cycle of El Niño, followed by La Niña, was particularly destructive.

~ ~

WHEN DOES LA NIÑA OCCUR?

Like El Niño, La Niña occurs irregularly, every few years. La Niña is less common than El Niño, occurring only every two to ten years. But a La Niña can last for as long as two years.

Between these two extremes, you may begin to wonder, is there ever a "normal" year? Yes. Water temperatures in the central Pacific swing back and forth, between the very warm conditions (El Niño), normal conditions, and cold conditions (La Niña). In the past half-century, El Niños have occurred 31 percent of the time and La Niñas 23 percent of the time. There were twenty-three El Niños in the 1900s, but only fifteen La Niñas.

~ ~

CLIMATE SURPRISE

In May and June of 1998, scientists suspected that a La Niña was beginning to develop when ocean temperatures in the central Pacific fell below normal. They knew that during the La Niña of 1988–1989, which was a major one, Pacific surface water temperatures cooled 7°F (4°C) in two months. In 1998, the cooling was even more rapid. In one month, the water temperature dropped by 15°F (8°C).

Understandably, scientists were worried that the La Niña of 1998 would be a terribly strong one because ocean temperatures dropped so rapidly. But the trend did not continue. Temperatures in the tropical Pacific Ocean stayed moderately cold without becoming a large-scale La Niña. Many of the predicted effects of La Niña did not come about. Instead of colder-than-normal temperatures in the Northeast and Midwest, these areas had normal weather. Climatologists and meteorologists are investigating whether other factors may have counteracted some of La Niña's effects that year.

7
THE SCIENCE OF TRACKING EL NIÑO

After the disastrous El Niño of 1982–1983, scientists around the world began setting up systems to study El Niño. Today boats, buoys, and satellites equipped with scientific instruments beam information about ocean currents to scientists. Climatologists use high-speed computers to analyze this information. Using data from these tools, climatologists predicted the El Niño of 1997–1998 months ahead of time, so people had more time to prepare for it.

~ ~

MAPPING THE BUMPY OCEAN
Scientists monitor the development of El Niños using a variety of methods. The TOPEX/Poseidon satellite, a joint venture between the United States and France, measures sea levels. It bounces radar signals off the surface of the

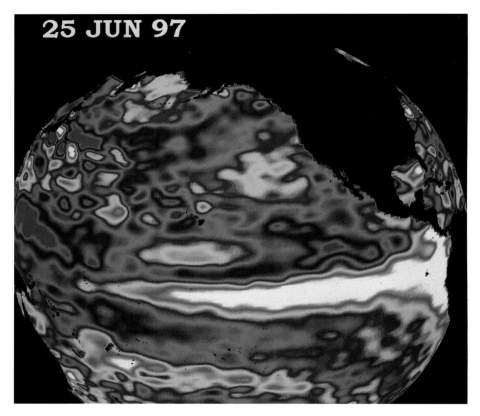

25 JUN 97

A TOPEX/Poseidon image of the Pacific Ocean, June 1997, shows El Niño conditions. The white and red areas show unusual patterns of warm water. In white areas the sea level is between 6 to 13 inches (14 to 32 centimeters) above normal, green areas represent normal sea conditions, and purple areas are at least 7 inches (18 centimeters) below normal sea level. Compare with the illustration on page 57.

ocean. By measuring how long it takes for the signals to bounce back to the satellite, scientists can figure out the distance from the satellite to the ocean, and thereby, sea level. They create a contour map of the ocean, much like

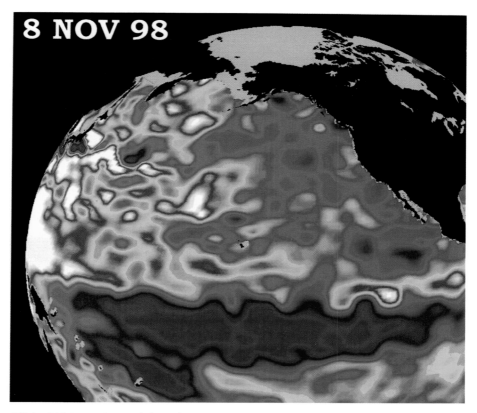

8 NOV 98

This TOPEX/Poseidon image shows La Niña conditions. Compare the locations of warm (red, white) and cold (purple) water with the TOPEX/Poseidon El Niño image and notice how warm water pooling against Asia differs from the pattern illustrated on page 56.

the contour maps that show peaks, valleys, and other features on land.

The surface of the ocean is bumpy, with subtle hills and valleys that indicate where currents lie. These hills of water are wind-driven. They are also influenced by ocean temperature. When seawater warms, its molecules become

A Tropical Atmosphere Ocean Array (TAO) buoy

more active and move farther apart. The warm water takes up more space, and bulges, causing a local rise in sea level. When ocean water cools, sea levels fall. By measuring and mapping sea levels every ten days, the TOPEX/Poseidon satellite can locate ocean currents and estimate their speed and direction. It can also monitor the size of the pool of warm water that forms in the Pacific Ocean during an El Niño.

Another climate tracking tool, run by the United States, France, Japan, Korea, and Taiwan, is the Tropical Atmosphere Ocean Array (TAO), a system of seventy buoys moored in the Pacific Ocean. These floats are equipped with sensors that monitor air temperature, air humidity, wind speed, wind direction, rainfall, ocean temperatures, and ocean currents. Stretching from Peru to

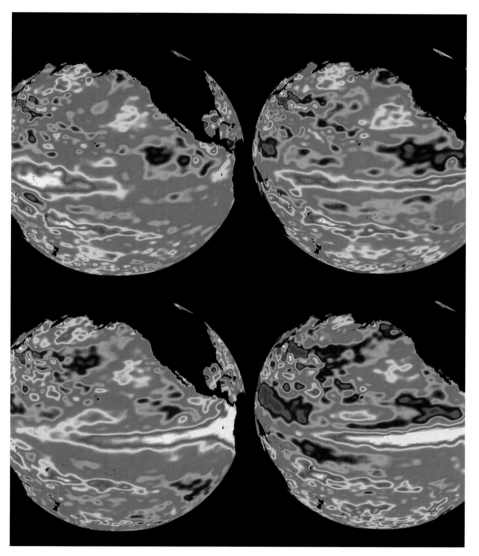

These four TOPEX/Poseidon images show changes in the
Pacific Ocean during the El Niño of 1997. From (left to right,
top to bottom) April 25, May 25, June 25, and September 5,
weakened trade winds let warmer water move eastward,
against the coast of Peru, below the black outline of North
and Central America.

Australia, the buoys beam information to satellites, which send it to scientists' computers. Data from the TAO buoys is supplemented by sensors on buoys that float freely in the ocean, and by data gathered by scientists on ships that crisscross the oceans. All this information is useful not only for day-to-day weather predictions, but also for computer models that help predict El Niños.

~ ~

WHY PREDICTIONS MATTER

Predicting and tracking El Niños can help people prepare for them, and so reduce loss of property and life. If people know a drought or rainy season is coming, they can gather supplies of food and medicine, move out of low-lying locations, and weatherproof their houses. They can plant the kinds of crops that do well in the predicted rainy or dry seasons. By stockpiling sandbags, clearing flood drainage canals, and weatherproofing houses, many Californians escaped damage from the heavy rains of El Niño 1997–1998. Preparations also helped save lives in Peru.

~ ~

COMPUTER CLIMATE MODELS:
WOW, CLIMATE'S COMPLEX!

A computer model is a program that uses mathematics to imitate something real. For a computer climate model, which imitates Earth's climate, climatologists input air temperatures, ocean temperatures, and other such information into the computer program. That gives the computer a picture of Earth's present climate conditions. Following a set of rules that imitate the way the ocean and atmosphere work, the programs make predictions about how today's climate patterns will change in the future. Scientists can then find out whether these conditions will likely lead to an El Niño, a La Niña, or normal conditions.

Earth's climate is very complex and difficult to model. A small change in the initial conditions can drastically shift the outcome. Imagine you are a scientist creating a program to predict Earth's climate. Below are just a few of the many weather-influencing processes you would need to incorporate into your weather-predicting program.

• *The Sun heats Earth unevenly.* Uneven heating occurs for many reasons. Because the Sun shines most directly on the equator, the equatorial areas receive more of the Sun's energy per square inch than the polar areas. Land heats up and cools off more quickly than water. So air over land shifts temperature more often and more rapidly than air over water. Another reason Earth is unevenly heated is that snowy and icy places bounce much of the Sun's energy back into space. As a result, those areas stay very cool. Because of these and other factors, air and water temperatures vary all over the planet.

• *Earth rotates.* As Earth rotates, it drags along the atmosphere. It stirs winds and ocean currents, affecting their movement and direction. Because of Earth's rotation, only half of the planet is facing the sun and being heated at a given time. The other half is colder and experiencing night. This contributes to the uneven heating of Earth.

• *Air masses move.* Warm air and cold air don't stay in place. (If they did, the poles would be much colder and the tropics would be much hotter than they are.) Warm air, which is less dense, tends to rise. Cold air, which is more dense, tends to fall. Every day, all over Earth, large masses of warm and cold air shift, almost as if they were jostling for position.

• *Air tends to flow from places of high pressure to places of low pressure.* Air tends to flow from high-pressure areas to low-pressure areas, creating wind. Changes in air pressure drive the movement of weather systems. The arrival of a high-pressure system over an area usually means the weather will be stable. Low-pressure areas are marked by clouds and storms.

• *Winds blow.* Earth has many winds. Trade winds, westerlies, and polar easterlies are all prevailing winds, winds that blow generally in one direction. There are also many other winds, including the jet stream.

• *Water moves in a complex cycle.* Earth's water is constantly moving, and changing from solid to liquid to gas. It evaporates from the surface of the ocean, from lakes and rivers, from puddles and even off of wet leaves. Up in the atmosphere, it cools and condenses, changing from gas to liquid, forming clouds and rain. It also freezes into snow and ice. As water changes form, it takes up or releases heat. This affects the temperature of surrounding air and water.

• *Ocean currents constantly move.* Masses of cold and warm ocean water are constantly shifting position, affecting the temperature and the moisture content of the air above them.

• *Landscape features affect winds and weather.* Air movement is affected by mountains, valleys, and other land features. For instance, mountains can not only block air movement or channel winds into valleys, they can

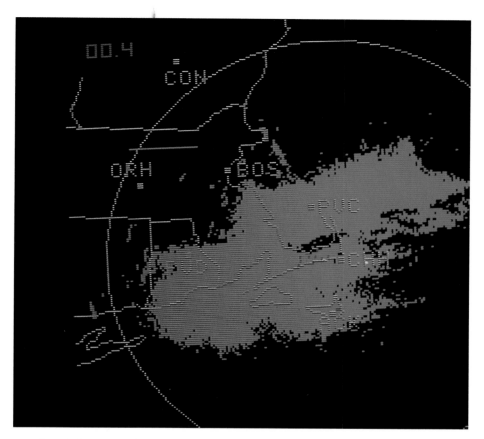

A cloud front moving across New England in a computer-generated weather forecasting program

affect air temperatures and trigger rains by causing air to move up over them. Moist air blown toward a mountain is forced up the slopes to higher altitudes, where it is cooled. Cold air holds less water vapor than warm air. So the cooled air drops some of its load of moisture as rain.

The aspects of weather and climate mentioned here are only some of the variables scientists must plan for in

OTHER MAJOR PLAYERS

El Niño and La Niña are not the only factors that influence climate in the United States. Air over the North Atlantic Ocean seesaws between different conditions of atmospheric pressure, switching every decade or so. This cycle, called the North Atlantic Oscillation, has a strong influence on climate in Europe and North America. Scientists do not yet understand how it works, but it may be linked to ocean currents, as ENSO is.

Lately, meteorologists are also having to consider another pattern in their predictions: a general warming of the areas they have studied in the northern and eastern United States. Since the 1960s, meteorologists have noticed a gradual increase in average air temperatures across the United States, especially in winter. In 1998–1999, this overall warming may have counteracted some of the wintertime cooling that La Niña usually causes. That winter, temperatures in the northern states were average or higher than normal, not as cold as would have been expected during a La Niña year. Scientists may be able to predict, though not perfectly, El

their computer models. In this swirling, whirling mass of change, scientists try to identify patterns. Sometimes they are successful; sometimes they are not. Each year, scientists use computer models to predict the year's climate. Then, when they see what actually happens that year, they adjust their computer models to make them more and more realistic.

8 LOOKING BACK TO SEE THE FUTURE

El Niños aren't new. Scientists have discovered evidence that El Niño events have occurred many times in the past. To find out about past climate, scientists read diaries, logbooks, and records kept by fishermen, explorers, and anyone else who kept an eye on the weather. They look for references to unusual rains, floods, or the amount of fish caught in a certain year. Journals kept by Spanish colonists in Peru mention El Niño as far back as 1525. Information about past El Niños is important because it shows climatologists the patterns of El Niño. Knowing more about El Niño's patterns will help people better forecast and prepare for future El Niños.

~ ~

TREES TELL THE STORY
It's not only people who record the effects of El Niño. Evidence of El Niño has also been found in trees, corals,

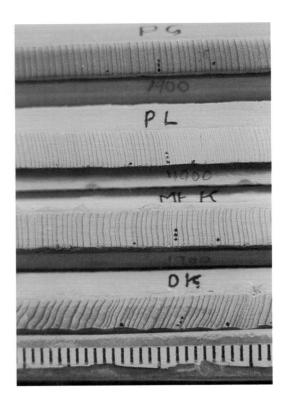

These tree cores have been dried and glued to a backing so they can be easily examined. Three dots show a century (1900), and single dots mark ten-year intervals.

and even glacial ice. Dendrochronologists are scientists who learn about the past by studying tree rings, the rings you see on the stump of a tree. In spring, when a tree grows quickly, it forms light-colored wood. In summer it grows denser, darker wood. On a stump, a light ring and a dark ring together form the record of one year of tree growth. A wide band indicates it was a good year for growth, with plenty of rain and sun and warmth. A narrow band may indicate a dry year, when trees grew slowly.

To study tree rings, dendrochronologists look at the stumps of dead trees or at small, strawlike cores drilled from the trunks of living trees. Tree rings of fir trees in

Mexico and bristlecone pines in the southwestern United States have thick bands, indicating wet years, about every five years in the 20th century. These coincide with El Niño years, when those areas would have experienced wet weather. Trees such as bristlecone pines can live thousands of years, so their rings can give dendrochronologists clues about the distant past. Rings of trees in Arizona and Chile indicate a strong El Niño occurred almost 1,000 years ago.

~ ~

CORALS CONFIRM IT

Like trees, corals grow each year and leave a record behind. A cross section of coral has noticeable layers. A thick layer indicates a good year for coral growth—the water was the right temperature for corals to grow. In very warm or cold years, however, growth is slower, or some of the corals may die. During El Niño years, when the water is very warm near the Galapagos Islands, corals there do not grow well; they have thinner growth layers. So scientists can find evidence of past El Niños by taking coral samples. Coral reefs in the Galapagos Islands show that a very strong El Niño occurred in the early 1600s, crippling coral growth.

~ ~

ANCIENT ICE HOLDS MORE CLUES

To look back even farther into history, scientists study glacial ice. Glaciers are tremendous riverlike masses of ice that form from snow that falls over thousands of years. The weight of snow on top presses on the snow

The Quelccaya ice cap ends in a spectacular 180-feet (55-meter) -high cliff. The layers you see are 1.5 feet (.75 meter) thick. It's easy to date them because dust during the annual dry season leaves a dark band. As newer layers bury older layers, snow under pressure turns into ice—layers at the bottom, 538 feet (164 meters) down, have been compressed to 1.5 inches (4 centimeters) thick.

beneath, which turns it into ice. Climatologists drill down into the ice to bring up giant, cylindrical ice cores. They contain ice layers that formed years ago. The sizes of the ice layers give climatologists information about what happened in a certain year. A wet year, for instance, would mean more snowfall, and therefore a thicker layer of ice.

A drought leaves a thinner layer of ice. The ice also might be dusty from soil blowing off dry land in a drought year.

In 1983, high in the mountains of Peru, scientists drilled down into a glacier and brought up a core containing ice as much as 1,500 years old. The ice layers clearly showed that Peru had experienced cycles of wet and dry climate for centuries. Some of these extreme climatic events almost surely reflect strong El Niños.

Archaeologists, scientists who study remains of past human life and activities, were very interested in the ice cores. They had been studying the ruins of the Moche civilization, which existed along Peru's coast from A.D. 100 to 800. By looking at Moche ruins and at the timing of droughts and floods indicated by the ice cores, archaeologists now understand more about how the Moche civilization grew and declined. They believe that droughts and El Niño episodes probably contributed to crop failures and floods that may have led to the collapse of the Moche civilization. Archaeologists are also studying how climate changes have affected civilizations such as the Maya of Mexico, the Anasazi of the southwestern United States, and the ancient Egyptians.

TAKING THE SPIN OFF

If you're still thinking El Niño is no big deal, consider this: the 1997–1998 El Niño actually made Earth rotate more slowly! El Niño shifted the direction of the trade winds and strengthened the jet stream, making the atmosphere move more quickly in the direction Earth rotates. To compensate and keep its overall momentum constant, Earth rotated more slowly, adding a tiny fraction of a second to each day that year. Earth's rotation speeded up again when La Niña began.

IS THE CLIMATE CHANGING?

Each year, even in a non–El Niño year, people think some weather events are odd, or unusual, or surprising. It seems like the climate is changing. But is it really? Climatologists and farmers and weathermen—and many others—would like to know.

Today there is a lot of scientific debate about how long El Niños have been occurring, and whether they are becoming more frequent or more intense. So far, by studying corals and glacial ice, climatologists have discovered evidence of El Niños as far back as five thousand years. Tree rings indicate that before 1880, El Niños only occurred about once every seven and a half years. Since then, El Niños have arrived about one every four years. Just looking at this part of history, it seems that El Niños are becoming more frequent. In the same period, La Niñas have become less frequent.

Does this indicate a fundamental change in Earth's climate, or just a short-term fluctuation? At present, it's impossible to know. To study climate trends, climatologists prefer to look at the "big picture"—the behavior of climate over many hundreds or thousands of years. Will El Niños become even more frequent? Will they continue occurring about once every 4 years? No one knows.

GLOBAL WARMING AND EL NIÑO

Many scientists are looking for a link between El Niños and global warming, the gradual overall warming of Earth's atmosphere. Earth *is* warming. In the past fifty years, Earth's average daily air temperature has risen 0.9°F (0.5°C). The warmest year of the century so far was 1997. Glaciers are melting. Antarctic ice is melting and becoming unstable.

Most, but not all, scientists think that the increasing buildup of greenhouse gases is causing global warming. Greenhouse gases—such as water vapor, methane, and carbon dioxide—trap heat from sunlight in Earth's atmosphere the way glass walls trap heat in a greenhouse. (The same thing occurs when the inside of a car heats up on a sunny day.) Coal-burning factories, gasoline engines in automobiles and lawn mowers, and burning forests release greenhouse gases that can contribute to global warming.

According to climatologists' predictions, global warming probably won't be felt equally all over Earth. Climate patterns are likely to shift, with some areas becoming warmer, some cooler, some wetter, and some drier than today. How this will effect the El Niño Southern Oscillation is uncertain. Will more heat mean more unstable weather and more El Niños? At least one prominent climatologist believes this will be the case. So far, however, most climatologists do not think there is enough evidence to confirm such a link. They believe it is much too early to assume El Niños will increase as Earth warms. Earth's atmosphere and oceans are a complex and wondrous system that scientists are only beginning to understand.

RESOURCES

BOOKS AND PERIODICALS

* Arnold, Caroline. *El Niño: Stormy Weather for People and Wildlife.* New York: Clarion, 1998.

Benchley, Peter. "Galapagos: Paradise in Peril," *National Geographic,* April 1999, pp. 2–31.

Canby, T.Y. "El Niño's Ill Wind," *National Geographic,* February 1984, pp. 144–183.

Fagan, Brian. *Floods, Famines, and Emperors: El Niño and the Fate of Civilizations.* New York: Basic Books, 1999.

Glantz, Michael. *Currents of Change: El Niño's Impact on Climate and Society.* New York: Cambridge University Press, 1996.

Suplee, Curt. "El Niño-La Nina: Nature's Vicious Cycle," *National Geographic,* March 1999, pp. 73–95.

* for younger readers

WEB SITES

The Web is full of El Niño sites. Just search for keyword el niño. (You do not need the accent over the n to find these sites.) Web sites come and go, but here are a few good ones available at the time this book goes to press:

www.esig.ucar.edu
El Niño glossary can be accessed through their search engine. This glossary clarifies the meaning of El Niño–related terms.

www.pbs.org/wgbh/nova/elnino
Tracking El Niño NOVA site
This site, set up by the people who produce NOVA television specials for WGBH Boston, has many pages of clear, interesting articles, diagrams, and photos about the history of El Niño and how it affects weather.

http://www.ala.org/acrl/resoct98.html
El Niño Site Listings
This site, set up by the Association of College and Research Libraries, lists and describes most of the El Niño sites and has links to them.

http://www.tor.ec.gc.ca/elnino/index_e.cfm
El Niño in Canada
This site, provided by Environment Canada, shows the specific impacts of El Niño on Canada.

http://www.elnino.noaa.gov/lanina_new_faq.html
La Niña Frequently Asked Questions
Part of a site run by the U.S. National Oceanic and Atmospheric Administration, this gives a good introduction to La Niña.

GLOSSARY

climatologist: a scientist who studies a region's long-term weather conditions.

current: water that moves horizontally and whose movement is unrelated to tides.

dendrochronologist: a scientist who studies tree rings for clues about the past.

drought: a long period without precipitation.

El Niño: a warm surface current that periodically appears flowing along the coast of Peru. The term El Niño is also used in a more general way to describe both the oceanic and atmospheric events that occur along with the appearance of the warm current.

El Niño Southern Oscillation (ENSO): a term scientists use to describe the full range of oceanic and atmospheric conditions from El Niño years to normal years to La Niña years.

equator: the line that runs around Earth's middle, the place where Earth rotates at greatest speed.

floodplain: the area covered with water when a river floods.

glacier: a large mass of slow-moving ice.

global warming: the overall rise in Earth's air temperature, caused by a buildup of greenhouse gases, such as carbon dioxide, in the atmosphere.

greenhouse effect: the warming of Earth's climate caused by the trapping of ultraviolet radiation from the Sun by greenhouse gases within the atmosphere.

greenhouse gases: gases in Earth's atmosphere that contribute to the greenhouse effect. Carbon dioxide, water vapor, and methane are greenhouse gases.

hurricane: a severe tropical cyclone with winds over 74 miles per hour (115 kilometers per hour).

jet streams: fast moving rivers of air that flow 10 to 15 miles (16 to 24 kilometers) above Earth and affect the position of weather systems. Jet streams occur in the Southern and Northern hemispheres.

La Niña: the term given to ocean conditions that are the opposite of those in an El Niño year. During a La Niña, a large pool of colder-than-average ocean water spreads to the central Pacific Ocean. La Niña is also called El Viejo or a cold event.

meteorologist: a scientist who studies the atmosphere and weather.

monsoon: a seasonal reversal of wind direction that brings rain to the Asian mainland.

North Atlantic Oscillation: seesawing atmospheric conditions, probably influenced by the ocean, that strongly affect weather in Europe and eastern North America.

Southern Oscillation: the seesawing conditions of high pressure and low pressure air that occur over the Pacific Ocean.

teleconnection: a link between unusual climate events in widely separated parts of the world.

thermocline: the division in water layers where a warmer, oxygen-rich surface layer is separated from a colder oxygen-poor bottom layer.

trade winds: winds that blow generally east to west, toward the equator, from latitudes 30° north and south of the equator. (They are called trade winds because sailing ships carrying cargo for trade once used these winds to push them from Europe toward the Americas.)

upwelling: the rising of cold, deep ocean water to the ocean's surface.

INDEX

Page numbers in *italics* refer to illustrations.

Africa, 49, 50
air pollution, 46
air pressure, 11, 13, 14, 39, *49*, 50–52
algae, 23
Amazon rain forest, 26, *28*, 29
Anasazi, 69
anchovies, 20
Anthony, June, *15*
archaeologists, 69
Asia, 11–13, 16, 46–48
Atacama Desert, 30–31
Atlantic Ocean, 36, 64
atmospheric (air) pressure, 11, 13, 14, 39, *49*, 50–52
Australia, 13, 23, *49*, 50, *52*, 53

Baja California, 10, 34, 36
barometer, 13
bleached coral, 23
Botswana, *15*
Brazil, 26, 27, *28*

California, 10, 18, 21, 32–36, *33*, *35*, 44–45, *45*
Canada, 40, 42
carbon dioxide, 71
Cardiff, California, 35
Caribbean Islands, 37
Chile, 19, 21, 26, 30–31, 53
Chimalapas rain forest, 40, *41*
climatologists, 60, 65, 68, 70
computer climate models, 60–64, *63*
corals, 9, 22–23, 67, 70

Death Valley, California, 32
deep ocean water, 12, 16, 17
deforestation, 29
dendrochronologists, 66–67
dengue fever, 30
deserts, 9, 30–32, 34, 42–43
disease, 29–30
drought, 9, *15*, 27, 48, 50, 53

Earth, rotation of, 61, 69
earthquakes, 18
Ecuador, 10, 19, 21, 23, 26

Egyptians, ancient, 69
El Niño
    in Asia, 46–48
    coral reefs and, 22–23
    deaths and damage caused by,
        18, 26, 32, *33*, 34, 35,
        37–38, 43–44
    defined, 10
    disease and, 29–30
    fishing and, 10–12, 19–21
    Galapagos Islands and, 21,
        23–25
    global warming and, 70–71
    in history, 65–70
    in North America, 32–45
    predicting, 18, 55–64
    in South America, 26–31
    strength of, 18
    TOPEX/Poseidon image of, *56,
        59*
    web sites, 73–74
El Niño Southern Oscillation
    (ENSO), 13, 64, 71
El Viejo (*see* La Niña)
equator, 26, 39, 52
evaporation, 17

Federal Emergency Management
    Administration, 44
fishing, *10*, 10–12, 19–21
floodplain, 27
floods, 9, 18, 26, 27, 40, 44
Florida, 37–38, *38*
forest fires, 27, *28*, 29, 40, *41*,
    46–48, *47*
fossil hunters, 34
freezing rain, 40

Galapagos Islands, 21, 23–25,
    67
Georgia, 39
glacial ice, 67–70, *68*
global warming, 64, 70–71
greenhouse effect, 71

greenhouse gases, 71
Gulf Coast, 37
Guyana, 27

hantavirus, 30
Hurricane Linda, 36, *37*
hurricanes, 36–37, *37*, 52,
    53

Incas, 28
India, 49, 50
Indian Ocean, 49–50
Indonesia, 46–48, 53
insects, 43
Irian Jaya, 48

Java, 48
jet stream, 37–39, *49*, *52*, 53,
    62, 69

Kissimmee, Florida, *38*

Laguna Beach, California, 32
land iguanas, 23, 25
La Niña
    defined, 14
    effects of, 53
    occurrences of, 53–54
    strength of, 18
    TOPEX/Poseidon image of,
        57

malaria, 30
marine iguanas, 23, *24*
Maya, 69
meteorologists, 64
methane, 71
Mexico, 35, 36, 40, *41*
Minnesota, 42
Moche civilization, 69
Mojave Desert, 34, 42
monsoons, 12, 13, 50
mosquitoes, 30
mud slides, 26, 29, 32, 34, 53

North America, 32–45
North Atlantic Oscillation, 64
North Carolina, 39, 40

ocean currents, 10–11, 14, 58, 62
ocean temperatures, 10–11, 13, 14, 23, 52, 54, 57–58

Pacifica, California, *35*
Pacific Ocean, 10–12, 16–18, 48, 51
Papua New Guinea, 48
pelicans, 19, 23
penguins, 23, 24
Peru, 9–13, *10*, 18, 19, 20–21, 26–30, *37*, 53, 65, 69
phytoplankton, 19, *20*
plants, 9, 11, 24–25, 31, 32, 42–43
polar easterlies, 62
prevailing winds, 62

Quelccaya ice cap, *68*

rainfall, 12–13, 24, 26, 27, 30–34, 39, 48

San Francisco, California, 32
Santa Monica, California, 32
seabirds, 19, 21, 24, 25
sea lions, 21, *22*, 23–25
seals, 21
settlements, in risky areas, 28, 29, 44–45
sewage systems, 30
slash-and-burn agriculture, 29, 46
snow, 9, 36, 42
soil, 27, 29
Sonora Desert, 42
South America, 16, 26–31
  Chile, 19, 21, 26, 30–31, 53

Ecuador, 10, 19, 21, 23, 26
  Peru, 9–13, *10*, 18, 19, 20–21, 26–30, *37*, 53, 65, 69
  Venezuela, 30
South Carolina, 39
Southern Oscillation, 13, 64, 71
starvation, 21
Sun, 11, 61
sunspots, 18
surface ocean water, 12, 16, 17
surfing, 35–36

Tahiti, 13, *49*, *52*
teleconnections, 49–50
Tennessee, 40
thermocline, 16, 17
TOPEX/Poseidon satellite, 55–58, *56*, *57*, *59*
tornadoes, 37–38, *38*, 53
tortoises, 23, *24*
trade winds, 11, 12, 14, 16, 17, *49*, *52*, 62, 69
tree rings, 66–67, 70
Tropical Atmosphere Ocean Array (TAO) buoys, *58*, 58, 60

upwelling, 19, 52

Venezuela, 30
volcanoes, 18

water vapor, 71
waves, 34–36
web sites, 73–74
westerlies, 62
Wilmot, Lloyd, *15*
winds, 11–14, 16, 17, *49*, *52*, 62, 69

zooplankton, 19, *20*
zooxanthellae, 23